Giant Machines

web linked

Giant
Machines

By Steve Parker
Illustrated by Alex Pang

First published in 2010 by Miles Kelly Publishing Ltd
Harding's Barn, Bardfield End Green, Thaxted, Essex, CM6 3PX, UK

Copyright © Miles Kelly Publishing Ltd 2010

10 9 8 7 6 5 4 3 2 1

Editorial Director: *Belinda Gallagher*
Art Director: *Jo Brewer*
Design Concept: *Simon Lee*
Volume Design: *Rocket Design*
Cover Designer: *Simon Lee*
Indexer: *Gill Lee*
Production Manager: *Elizabeth Collins*
Reprographics: *Stephan Davis*
Consultants: *John and Sue Becklake*

All rights reserved. No part of this publication may be reproduced,
stored in a retrieval system, or transmitted by any means, electronic,
mechanical, photocopying, recording or otherwise, without the prior
permission of the copyright holder.

ISBN 978-1-84810-284-2

Printed in China

British Library Cataloguing-in-Publication Data
A catalogue record for this book is available from the British Library

Every effort has been made to acknowledge the source and copyright
holder of each picture. Miles Kelly Publishing apologises for any
unintentional errors or omissions.

MADE WITH PAPER FROM
A SUSTAINABLE FOREST

ACKNOWLEDGEMENTS

All panel artworks by Rocket Design
The publishers would like to thank the following
sources for the use of their photographs:
Alamy: 25 Jim Parkin; 28 Jim West
Corbis: 6(t) Bettmann, (c) Patrick Pleul/dpa
Dreamstime: 9 Vladikpod; 11 Orientaly; 17 Orangeline;
27 Amaranta
Fotolia: 18 Paul Fearn; 20 Jose Gil
Getty Images: 30, 32 AFP
iStock: 23 Joe Gough
Photolibrary: 7(c); 13 Glow Images; 20 Con Tanasiuk;
35 Bernd Laute
Rex Features: 14 Nicholas Bailey; 36 Paul Grover
Science Photo Library: 7(r) Ria Novosti
All other photographs are from Miles Kelly Archives

WWW.FACTSFORPROJECTS.COM

Each top right-hand page directs
you to the Internet to help you
find out more. You can log on
to **www.factsforprojects.com**
to find free pictures, additional
information, videos, fun activities
and further web links. These
are for your own personal use
and should not be copied or
distributed for any commercial
or profit-related purpose.

If you do decide to use the
Internet with your book, here's a
list of what you'll need:
• A PC with Microsoft® Windows®
XP or later versions, or a
Macintosh with OS X or later,
and 512Mb RAM

• A browser such as Microsoft®
Internet Explorer 8, Firefox 3.X
or Safari 4.X
• Connection to the Internet via
a modem (preferably 56Kbps) or
a faster Broadband connection
• An account with an Internet
Service Provider (ISP)
• A sound card for listening to
sound files

Links won't work?
www.factsforprojects.com is
regularly checked to make sure
the links provide you with lots
of information. Sometimes you
may receive a message saying
that a site is unavailable. If this
happens, just try again later.

Stay safe!
When using the Internet, make
sure you follow these guidelines:
• Ask a parent's or a guardian's
permission before you log on.
• Never give out your personal
details, such as your name,
address or email.
• If a site asks you to log in or
register by typing your name
or email address, speak to your
parent or guardian first.
• If you do receive an email from
someone you don't know, tell
an adult and do not reply to the
message.
• Never arrange to meet anyone
you have talked to on the
Internet.

Miles Kelly Publishing is not
responsible for the accuracy or
suitability of the information on
any website other than its own.
We recommend that children are
supervised while on the Internet
and that they do not use Internet
chat rooms.

www.mileskelly.net
info@mileskelly.net

Self-publish your
children's book

buddingpress.co.uk

CONTENTS

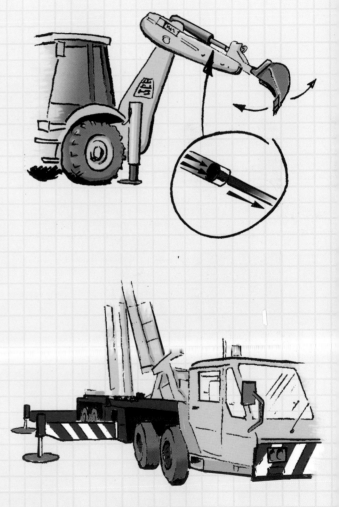

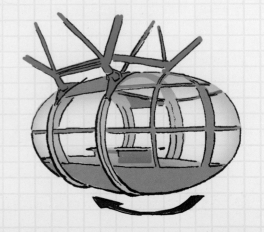

INTRODUCTION

Is bigger always better? Yes – and no. Giant machines do more work more quickly than small ones, saving time and effort. They are often more efficient, using less fuel to carry out more work. Also, sheer size is impressive. It encourages people to buy or hire massive machinery, and it may cause concern for their business rivals. There are drawbacks, however. Mobile giants are difficult to move along small roads, through narrow tunnels and over weak bridges. And if a giant breaks down, its parts are more expensive to buy and bring to the site.

This steam tractor from 1890, loaded with coal and water, was too big and heavy to catch on.

METAL TAKES OVER

In ancient Greece and Rome, early big machines were large cranes, levers, and catapults for warfare. They were mostly made from wood with a few small metal parts. During the 1700s, as the Industrial Revolution got under way, engineers developed ways of making huge metal parts from iron, and later from steel.

Immense excavators gobble up thousands of tonnes of rocks daily.

SUPER POWERS

People and animals powered the first large machines and vehicles. But you need far more force to power something as big as a house. The Industrial Revolution, which took place in the late 18th and early 19th centuries, was based on steam engines. By 1900, petrol and diesel engines were taking over. Then enormous electric motors began to be used. The biggest trucks, construction machines and railway locomotives are powered by diesel-electric systems.

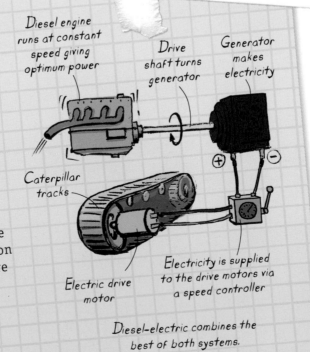

Diesel engine runs at constant speed giving optimum power

Drive shaft turns generator

Generator makes electricity

Caterpillar tracks

Electric drive motor

Electricity is supplied to the drive motors via a speed controller

Diesel-electric combines the best of both systems.

The machines featured in this book are Internet linked.
Visit www.factsforprojects.com to find out more.

AGE OF GIANTS

The world needs coal and oil for energy, as well as metals and other raw materials. People want bigger houses, shops and places to work, and more food. All of this means that machines such as excavators, dump trucks, bulldozers, cranes and harvesters become even more colossal. To build and maintain these mammoths needs new factories, service centres and delivery trucks for parts – which, in turn, means more giant machines.

Stabilizers emerge under hydraulic or electric motor power

Crane

Legs lower onto base plate feet to compress the ground

Squashy tyres are lifted off the ground to prevent swaying

Mobile cranes can lift tens of tonnes without toppling over.

How many wheels? Lots, as a multi-trailer truck delivers a vast grain silo (storage container).

ARE THERE LIMITS?

Just how big can machines and vehicles get? In the future our planet may suffer from energy shortages, pollution, climate change and other problems. This may affect the size of future machines.

Even space shuttles need a lift – from huge transport planes.

Perhaps the giant machines of today will one day give way to smaller, smarter versions.

BIGFOOT TRUCK

The 'Bigfoots' and similar monster trucks have been thrilling crowds since the 1970s. They are combinations, or hybrids, of a standard pick-up truck body such as the Ford F-250, with the suspension, drive shafts and axles from huge cargo or military vehicles. The giant 'flotation' tyres, such as those used on tractors and harvesters, are taller than a person, so the driver rides some 3 metres above the ground.

Eureka!

The original Bigfoot was built in 1975 by construction worker Bob Chandler, who liked to go off-roading at weekends. More trucks followed over the years. Some are for display, others are specialized for racing, jumps or stunts such as somersaults.

Whatever next?

Almost 20 official Bigfoot trucks have been built, and even bigger vehicles with massive mining dump-truck tyres are planned.

The Bigfoot Fastrax is based on a US Army M48 troop carrier with two 7.5-litre engines.

Exhaust manifold The tubes of the manifold collect exhaust gases from each cylinder and channel them to the exhaust pipes, one on each side.

Hand-held welding torch

Drive wheels push wire out of torch tip

Wire is one electrical contact, or electrode

Argon gas at torch tip shields the arc from the air

Supply of wire and argon are controlled by a finger trigger

Continuous metal spark or arc

Metal parts being welded are one electrical contact, or electrode

✳ How does WELDING work?

Welding joins metal parts by heating them to a very high temperature so that their edges almost melt and fuse. In gas welding, the heat is an incredibly hot flame from burning gas. In arc welding, the parts being welded are in an electrical pathway, along with a length of flexible filler wire that emerges slowly and steadily from the tip of the welding torch. When the wire touches the parts, it completes an electrical circuit and the electric current jumps across in the form of a very hot continuous spark called an arc. This melts the filler wire into the part edges like superhot glue.

Brakes The body of the Bigfoot does not weigh much, but when the heavy wheels and tyres spin, they need disc brakes to slow them.

Differential When steering around corners, this set of gears, the 'diff', allows the wheel on the outside of the curve to turn faster (see page 19).

The original Bigfoot series goes from 1 to 14. There is no Bigfoot 13 – due to the unlucky nature of this number!

To play an interactive Bigfoot game online, visit www.factsforprojects.com and click on the web link.

In 1999, Bigfoot 14 made a long jump of more than 61 m – over a Boeing 727 passenger jet.

Body Some Bigfoot-type trucks have the original steel body. Others have bodywork moulded from light, flexible, non-rusting GRP (glass-reinforced plastic) also known as fibre-glass.

A monster truck leaps over a school bus at its action-packed display

✳ It's the HIGH JUMP!

Bigfoots, monster trucks and similar huge vehicles put on special displays at race tracks and exhibition grounds. They compete against each other, sometimes with a handicap or drawback such as pulling a heavy trailer. They also have high-jump and long-jump competitions, or drive through hoops of fire. Emergency services, including an ambulance and fire appliance with cutting gear, stand by in case one of the trucks is crashed or crushed.

Rear diff

Tyre tread The tread grooves are usually cleaned of sand, mud, leaves and other debris with pressure-washers, to ensure a good grip.

Suspension Rows of shock absorbers (hydraulic dampers) allow the axles to tilt, jolt and vibrate, while keeping the body relatively stable so the driver can keep control.

Flotation tyres These massive tyres 'float' or stay on the surface of soft ground, rather than digging in like traction tyres. This allows them to maintain better grip – a traction tyre slips if it turns too fast.

Bigfoot's stunt of crushing old cars started as a joke in 1981.

The Grave Digger series of monster trucks is based on the 1950 Chevrolet Panel van. They have ghoulish scenes painted on the sides and the red headlights glow like a demon's eyes.

TRACTOR

The giant tractor is the endlessly adaptable 'workhorse' of the modern industrial farm. It pulls trailers loaded with all kinds of items, from hay bales to cattle or sheep. Its power take-off or PTO (see below), can connect to dozens of kinds of machines. Its huge diesel engine is heavy and noisy, but it is also reliable, powerful at low speeds and easy to adjust, service and repair.

The power of a big tractor engine is more than 750 horsepower – about the same as a Formula One racing car.

Eureka!

From the 1850s, working animals such as horses, oxen and buffalo were replaced by steam-driven traction engines, adapted from railway locomotives. Diesel- and petrol-engined tractors became popular from the 1900s.

Tractors have between three and six main gears, and also a range changer to alter these, so they can have more than 18 gear combinations.

Whatever next?

Simpler farming methods that are 'greener', causing less damage to the environment, are constantly being tested. Some farmers no longer plough fields, preferring to plant seeds straight into last year's surface.

The power take-off system was introduced in 1918, partly as a result of engineering research during World War I.

Power take-off The take-off coupling is usually at the rear of the tractor. But some types have a front coupling too, and even one to the side. However the tractor can only work one of these at a time.

Steps

✳ How does PTO work?

Power take-off (PTO) supplies a rotary or turning force from the tractor at a special joint, or coupling, usually at the vehicle's rear. All kinds of machines can be connected such as seed drills (planters), cutters, mowers, balers and spreaders for fertilizers or pesticides – meaning these machines do not need their own engines. The tractor tows the machine by a separate drawbar or hitch. The PTO is controlled by the driver through the gearbox, separately from the tractor's own wheels. So the tractor can be stationary while still supplying PTO. Most tractors also have connections to supply electricity and a hydraulic link.

Mudguard

PTO controls in tractor cab

PTO takes turning force from gearbox when engine is running

Rotating PTO shaft can be used to drive machinery

PTO coupling

Multi-wheels An extra outer wheel can be bolted to the inner wheel for very soft surfaces, then taken off to make the tractor narrower for road travel.

Discover facts and view photos of the world's biggest tractor by visiting www.factsforprojects.com and clicking on the web link.

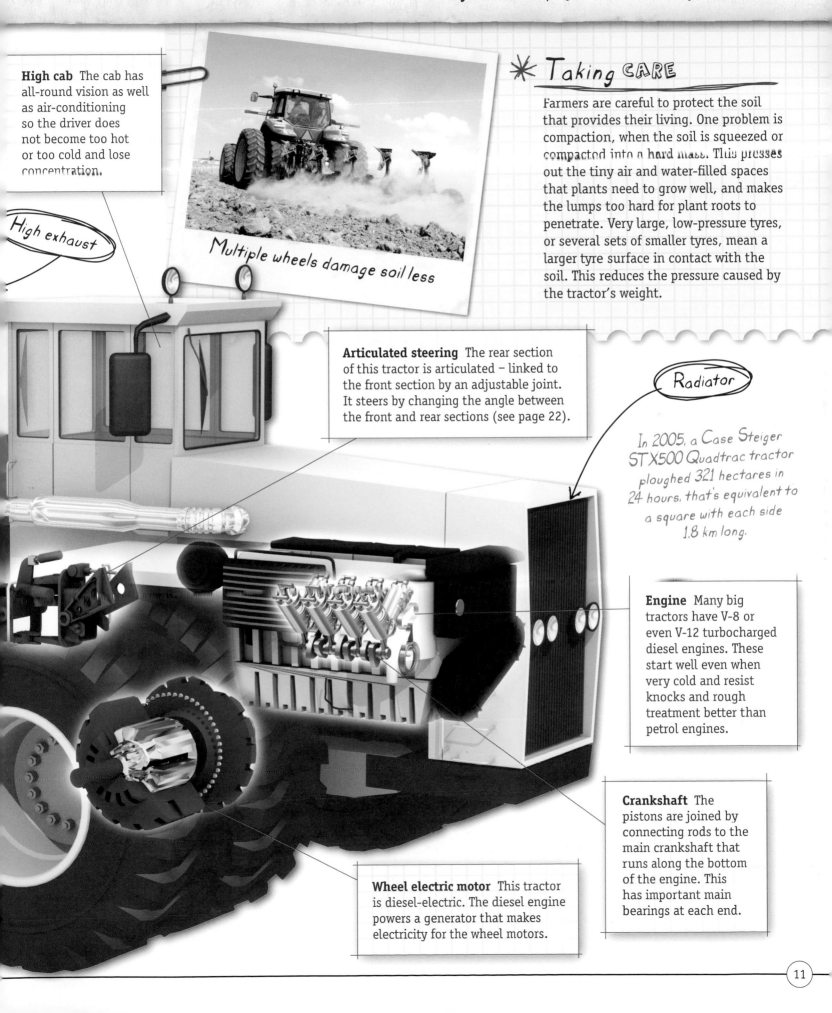

Multiple wheels damage soil less

High cab The cab has all-round vision as well as air-conditioning so the driver does not become too hot or too cold and lose concentration.

High exhaust

※ Taking CARE

Farmers are careful to protect the soil that provides their living. One problem is compaction, when the soil is squeezed or compacted into a hard mass. This presses out the tiny air and water-filled spaces that plants need to grow well, and makes the lumps too hard for plant roots to penetrate. Very large, low-pressure tyres, or several sets of smaller tyres, mean a larger tyre surface in contact with the soil. This reduces the pressure caused by the tractor's weight.

Articulated steering The rear section of this tractor is articulated – linked to the front section by an adjustable joint. It steers by changing the angle between the front and rear sections (see page 22).

Radiator

In 2005, a Case Steiger STX500 Quadtrac tractor ploughed 321 hectares in 24 hours, that's equivalent to a square with each side 1.8 km long.

Engine Many big tractors have V-8 or even V-12 turbocharged diesel engines. These start well even when very cold and resist knocks and rough treatment better than petrol engines.

Crankshaft The pistons are joined by connecting rods to the main crankshaft that runs along the bottom of the engine. This has important main bearings at each end.

Wheel electric motor This tractor is diesel-electric. The diesel engine powers a generator that makes electricity for the wheel motors.

COMBINE HARVESTER

The combine harvester combines the separate tasks of harvesting – cutting the crop and separating the valuable seeds or grains from less valuable parts, such as the straw (stalks) and chaff (dry cases around the grains). A modern combine harvester is the biggest and most expensive vehicle on the farm, doing the jobs of 100 people with its 10,000-plus moving parts, all driven by the big diesel engine.

Eureka!

During the 1800s, separate harvesting machines such as reapers and threshers were powered by animals, then steam engines, then tractors. The first self-powered combine harvesters were produced in the 1950s.

Whatever next?

Day by day, satellite photographs show farmers which parts of which fields are ready to harvest. The instructions are fed into the harvester's satnav or GPS so that it almost drives itself during its work.

Advanced combines not only have satnav (GPS) but also autopilot systems, like those on aircraft, to help the driver keep the machine straight on vast prairie-like fields.

Big combines measure more than 10 m long, 5 m wide and 4 m high. They weigh over 20 tonnes – and that's without their load of grain inside.

Forward cab The latest cabs are full of controls and displays, showing which parts of the combine are wearing and may need replacing.

1. Head's rotating reel pushes the crop down onto the cutter bar

4. Grains are separated and flow into tank or along tube

2. Blades cut or reap the crop

3. Threshing drum loosens the grains away from the stalks

5. Straw and chaff tumble from the rear (straw may be baled)

Cutter bar The very sharp cutter works like a hedge-trimmer to slice off the crop plant cleanly near to the ground, leaving a row of short stalks called stubble.

Controls

Tinted glass

Conveyor

✳ How do COMBINE HARVESTERS work?

For most grain crops, harvesting begins with reaping (cutting off the plants), which is carried out by the combine's reel-and-blade head. Next is threshing, when the seed grains are loosened from the unwanted parts, followed by winnowing, when the dry, light seed cases are blown away from the grains. The grains may be stored in the harvester's tank or blown along a pipe to a trailer pulled alongside by a tractor.

Reel Different reels or heads are used for different crops. These are usually various types of grain grasses, such as wheat, barley and rye.

Watch a video of a combine harvester at work by visiting www.factsforprojects.com and clicking on the web link.

Combine harvesters are expensive. For smaller farms, or those with few crop fields, it may be best to hire a combine and its driver, or to club together into a cooperative and buy one to share.

✳ Mechanized FARMING

Modern highly productive or 'intensive' farms rely on massive machines such as tractors, combine harvesters and spreaders. These use up vast resources of energy and materials to manufacture and run. However they harvest crops very quickly compared to simpler, less mechanical methods. Less of the crop is unripe or overripe and so less is wasted.

Vast fields are harvested by combine 'armies' when the grains are ripest

Unloader pipe The grains are blown by high-pressure air from a powerful fan out of the unloader pipe into a trailer.

Spreader This ejects and spreads the straw behind the combine.

Straw walkers These conveyors move the straw and other unwanted parts to the rear of the combine, for spreading or baling.

Steps

Threshing drums The rotating drums shake and rattle the grains away from the stems, chaff and other bits of the crop plant.

Sieves The grains fall through the holes in the sieves to the base of the combine, where they are stored or moved into the combine's own storage tank.

Laser beams allow the combine to harvest on sloping fields, by sensing the tilt necessary for the reel at the front by up to 5 degrees to either side.

BACKHOE LOADER

No building site is complete without at least one digger, otherwise known as the backhoe loader. The 'loader' refers to the front bucket, which scoops big items from ground level up to the top of its reach. The 'backhoe' is the longer rear arm, which not only reaches up but also down below ground level. It can dig trenches with a selection of narrow buckets or hoes.

Eureka!

In the 1950s, the backhoe loader was an early success for UK engineering company J C Bamforth, which expanded into the US and worldwide from the 1960s. This is why these machines are also known as JCBs.

Whatever next?

Pushing a digger blade into earth takes lots of force. Engineers are testing blades that vibrate to shake the soil and loosen its particles, letting the blade cut in more easily.

Joseph Cyril Bamforth founded his company in 1945, at the end of World War II, to take advantage of the rebuilding boom after the war.

In 1948 JCB employed six people. Today they have more than 8000 workers.

Hydraulic rams Hydraulic liquid pumped into one side of the piston moves it one way, then liquid pumped into the other side forces it back again the opposite way.

Loader bucket
There are two main controls, one to raise and lower the bucket on its arms, and one to tilt its angle.

Engine

435 B

Three diggers show some fancy bucket work in their dance routine

✳ Diggers on HOLIDAY

It's not all hard, dirty work for backhoe loaders, earth scrapers, tipper trucks and other construction giants. Some makers show off their vehicles in a light-hearted way to gain feelgood publicity. JCB's 'Dancing Diggers' formation team demonstrate skills such as lifting the main vehicle off the ground by its buckets, spinning around on the spot and climbing a steep slope using the backhoe as a long-reach grasping claw. This also showcases the machine's power, abilities and safety aspects.

Teeth

The world's largest backhoe loader factory is at Ballabgarh, in northern India. This town is also home to India's Cement Research Institute.

Loader arms The loader bucket cannot be lowered much below ground level (see page 22). If it is set at 'zero' height and driven forwards, it works as a simple ground leveller.

Take a 360° tour of a backhoe loader by visiting
www.factsforprojects.com and clicking on the web link.

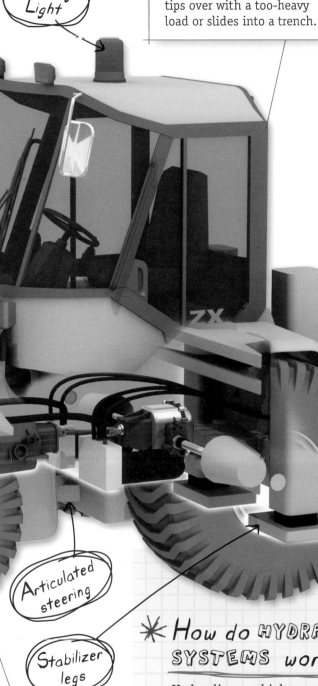

Flashing Light

Strengthened cab The cab has a strong safety frame in case the digger suddenly tips over with a too-heavy load or slides into a trench.

High-pressure hose The hydraulic fluid flows in and out of the ram cylinder through a thick-walled, high-pressure hose. This can bend as the sections of the arm change their angles.

Most backhoe loaders have headlights, indicators, speedometers and other equipment that allows them to drive on ordinary roads, from job to job.

Pivot

Push rods

Ram cylinder

Articulated steering

Stabilizer legs

Backhoe There are several sizes of hoe buckets, for digging trenches of different widths – narrow for pipes or cables, and broader for the concrete footings (foundations) of a building.

Low pressure tyres Huge tyres stop the digger slipping and sliding in the mud that gets everywhere on a construction site.

✳ How do HYDRAULIC SYSTEMS work?

Hydraulics use high-pressure liquids such as water or oil flowing in pipes and pushing against pistons, to move parts quite slowly but with enormous power. The pressure in the liquid is usually generated by the diesel engine. In the backhoe loader, each part of each arm has a piston and rod to push it one way, and then force it back again the other way, depending on which side of the piston the fluid pushes.

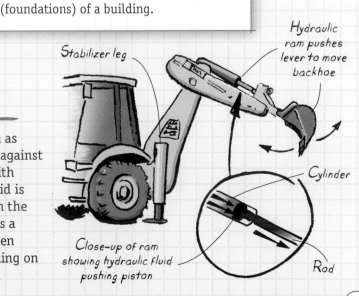

Stabilizer leg

Hydraulic ram pushes lever to move backhoe

Close-up of ram showing hydraulic fluid pushing piston

Cylinder

Rod

CONCRETE TRUCK

Thanks to the concrete truck there is no need for construction sites to store cement, sand, coarse aggregate (gravel-like stones), water and mixing machinery – all the components needed to make concrete. The ready-mix truck can carry several tonnes of concrete made to an exact recipe. Then it has to transport the mix to where it is needed within an hour or two, before the mix 'goes off' – sets as hard as rock.

If a concrete truck breaks down, or gets stuck in a traffic jam, its load hardens. Then it must be cleared out using road drills or even explosives.

Eureka!

Deliveries of already-mixed mortar and concrete began in the UK in the 1930s. The business expanded from the 1960s as more mixing centres meant that more customers could be reached before the mix hardened.

Whatever next?

Experiments are happening with concrete-type mixtures that stay softer for longer, hardening when exposed to powerful laser beams.

Drum The drum or barrel is turned by the truck's main engine, so the driver needs to keep on the move with little engine idling.

Loading chute The truck is loaded, or charged, with ingredients for the mix through this opening. The mix falls in from a tall container called a hopper at the concrete depot.

Discharge chute The mix flows out of this lower chute into whatever is waiting – a trench or hole, a concrete pump, or even wheelbarrows.

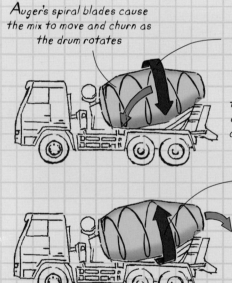

Auger's spiral blades cause the mix to move and churn as the drum rotates

With clockwise rotation the mix is pushed forwards into the base of the drum and keeps churning around

Anti-clockwise turning screws the mix rearwards, up and out of the drum, ready for use

Pivot

✳ How do AUGERS work?

An auger is a screw-like spiral or twisted structure that, when turned, drills into an object or material, or moves it along. Its basic design is like the Archimedes screw, used since ancient times to raise water from rivers into ditches. Big augers drill holes in the ground, raising the soil up and out. Another simple auger design is the corkscrew. The ready-mix drum has an auger, either a helical (coiled) blade on a central shaft, or spiral curved blades along the inside. As the drum spins, the blades mix and move the contents.

Concrete is measured in cubic metres, with a typical single measure weighing 2.5 tonnes.

View different models of concrete trucks and watch a video of one in action by visiting www.factsforprojects.com and clicking on the web link.

The first concrete trucks were developed in 1916 by Stephen Stepanian of Columbus, Ohio, USA.

✳ In the MIX

All concrete may look similar, but it is not. There are hundreds of ingredients, chemical additives and recipes for specialized mixes. These include recipes for very low or very high temperatures, enduring great weight or lots of vibrations, or for exposure to fresh or salty water. Concrete does not set by drying and losing water, but by a chemical reaction that depends on temperature. Keeping it cool helps to slow the hardening process.

Ready-mix pours from the chute into a footings trench for a building

Blades In this truck, sets of blades keep the mixture churning as the drum turns, to stop the mixture setting.

Water tank

Engine A powerful diesel engine turns the drum and/or the road wheels. An empty truck is less than half the weight of a full one, so the driver must adapt to the change.

Concrete mix

Multi-axles Several sets of wheels spread the huge weight, to stay within axle weight limits on ordinary roads and bridges.

Gearbox The engine can be disconnected from the road wheels so that it only drives the drum.

Big mixer trucks weigh 10–15 tonnes empty, and their loads are 10–20 tonnes.

DUMP TRUCK

On the building site, dumpers or tippers carry all kinds of objects – not only loose materials such as earth or rubble, but also huge pipes, girders and other heavy items. The dump truck needs a loader (see page 22), conveyor or similar machine to fill it up. But it can unload at the rear simply by raising, or tipping, its hinged body, called the bed or box.

Eureka!

The first dump trucks, modified from standard flat-bed trucks, were built in the 1920s in New Brunswick, Canada. The front end of the box was lifted by a winch and cable just behind the cab. By the 1930s they were spreading across North America and Europe.

The giant tipper trucks called 'centipedes' have a series of seven axles, rather than the usual two or three.

Diesel-electric dump trucks use powerful electric motors, like diesel-electric trains. This is more efficient than a diesel engine driving the road wheels through a complex system of gears, when much energy is lost.

A massive dumper takes on a load

✳ MONSTER dumpers

The biggest, roughest, toughest dumpers are used in mining and quarrying. They carry ores (rocks containing valuable substances such as metals) and similar loads away from the mine or quarry face, to long conveyors for loading onto road trucks or railway wagons. The latest robot dumpers use satnav (GPS) to follow their regular route within the mine or quarry site. Some can fit a whole house into the box, and cope with loads of 400-plus tonnes, making them among the largest of all vehicles.

Tailgate lip

Hydraulic rams These produce incredible force to lift the fully loaded box upwards as it tilts at the rear pivot. They work using high-pressure oil (see page 15).

Traction motor This diesel-electric truck has an enormously powerful electric motor for each road wheel. The motor turns very powerfully throughout its speed range (see page 33).

Chassis

To see lots more of pictures of dump trucks visit
www.factsforprojects.com and click on the web link.

Dump box The box is usually lightweight steel, so it is hard wearing but does not weigh too much.

Big tippers have cameras on the rear linked to a screen in the cab, so the driver can see exactly where to unload.

Cab

Generator Like a mini power station, this changes the turning force of the diesel engines into electric current for the traction motors in the road wheels.

Engines Really big dump trucks have two turbocharged diesel engines, one behind the other. They are coupled together so they both turn one shaft for the generator.

Cooling fan

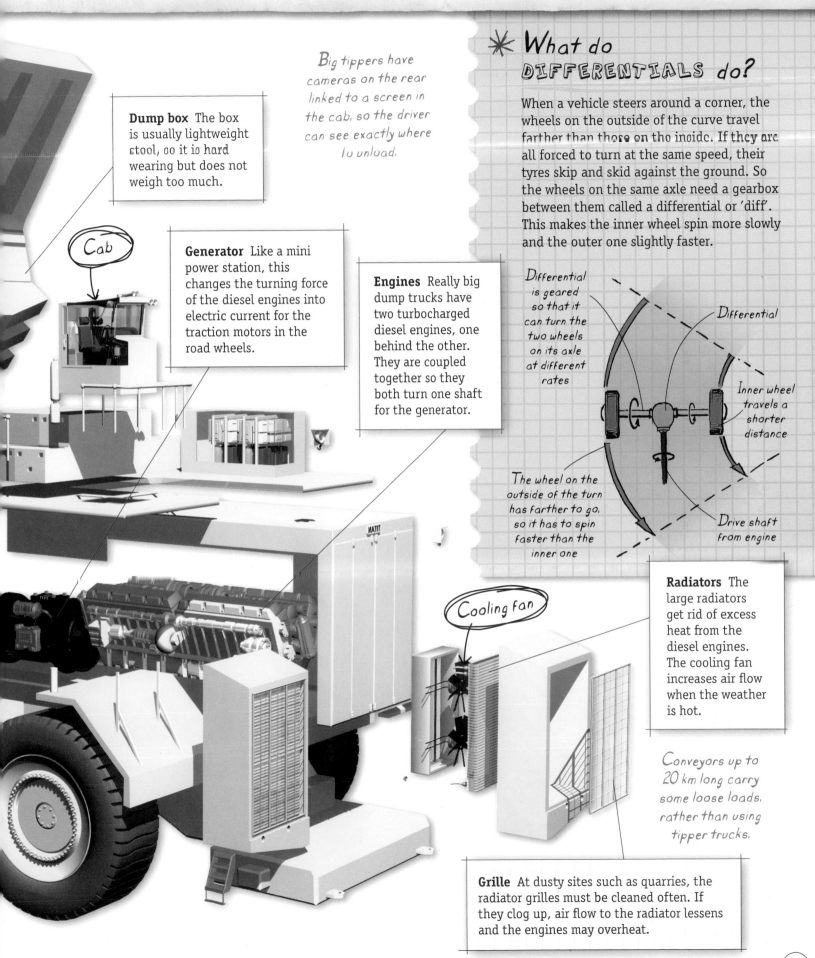

✱ What do DIFFERENTIALS do?

When a vehicle steers around a corner, the wheels on the outside of the curve travel farther than those on the inside. If they are all forced to turn at the same speed, their tyres skip and skid against the ground. So the wheels on the same axle need a gearbox between them called a differential or 'diff'. This makes the inner wheel spin more slowly and the outer one slightly faster.

Differential is geared so that it can turn the two wheels on its axle at different rates

Differential

Inner wheel travels a shorter distance

The wheel on the outside of the turn has farther to go, so it has to spin faster than the inner one

Drive shaft from engine

Radiators The large radiators get rid of excess heat from the diesel engines. The cooling fan increases air flow when the weather is hot.

Conveyors up to 20 km long carry some loose loads, rather than using tipper trucks.

Grille At dusty sites such as quarries, the radiator grilles must be cleaned often. If they clog up, air flow to the radiator lessens and the engines may overheat.

BULLDOZER

Often the biggest machine on the building site, and probably the heaviest, is the bulldozer or 'dozer. Its main task is to push loose material such as earth, sand or gravel, in order to spread it out and level the surface. Its crawler or caterpillar tracks spread its weight and prevent it slipping or sticking. The 'dozer's extraordinary push-pull power means that it can be called on for many tasks, including towing logs or rescuing vehicles that get stuck in the mud.

Eureka!

The first bulldozers were built in the 1920s in Kansas, USA. The term 'bull-dose' meant a large amount of very strong medicine to subdue a bull or similar large animal. It came into use for several big, powerful machines.

Whatever next?

Smaller, lighter bulldozers known as calfdozers are becoming more common for small building sites and to smooth snow for skiers.

Rear lights

Caterpillar's best-selling big D9 bulldozer weighs about 50 tonnes, while the giant D11 tips the scales at 100 tonnes.

✳ RIP it UP!

Very hard compacted soil or rubble, tarmac roads, concrete parking areas – none of these stand a chance against the bulldozer's ripper. Most 'dozers have one or more claw-like rippers at the rear that can be raised, lowered and angled like the blade. The ripper is pushed down through the hard surface, perhaps into a hole made by a road drill. Then the bulldozer uses its vast strength and tremendous weight to move along slowly, tearing up the material behind so it can be loosened further and collected or worked by other machines.

Caterpillar tracks
These are usually made of very hard rubber or metal. They consist of many linked parts called shoes or plates, or one long rubber belt with crosswise ridges.

FD14E
TURBO

The ripper claw tears up the ground for smoothing or clearing

Drive axle The axle turns the rear drive wheel for each track. The track's front wheel may not be driven and just rotates with the track.

Rear gearbox (diff) The fast rotation from the front gearbox is greatly slowed here, for the drive axles to move the tracks. In the process, the turning force (torque) increases hundreds of times, giving the bulldozer its tremendous power.

Watch an amazing video of bulldozers in action by visiting www.factsforprojects.com and clicking on the web link.

✳ How does the 'DOZER BLADE work?

Some bulldozers have a blade worked by strong steel cables that winch it up or down. But most use hydraulic arms to raise or lower the blade. Advanced bulldozers have a laser levelling system (see page 24) that measures the height of the blade and the 'dozer's body above a set point in the ground. The system automatically moves the blade to scrape the required surface perfectly flat or at a particular angle of slope.

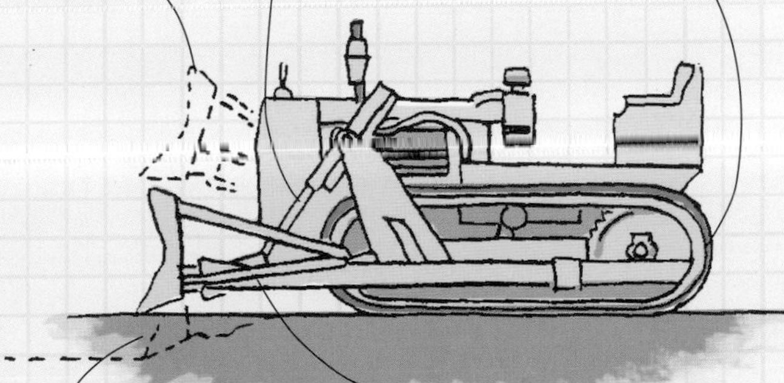

Blade in raised position

Hydraulic ram

Caterpillar tracks grip well and spread the 'dozers weight so it does not sink in

Depressing blade below ground level scoops out material

Reversing the 'dozer with blade lowered smooths the ground

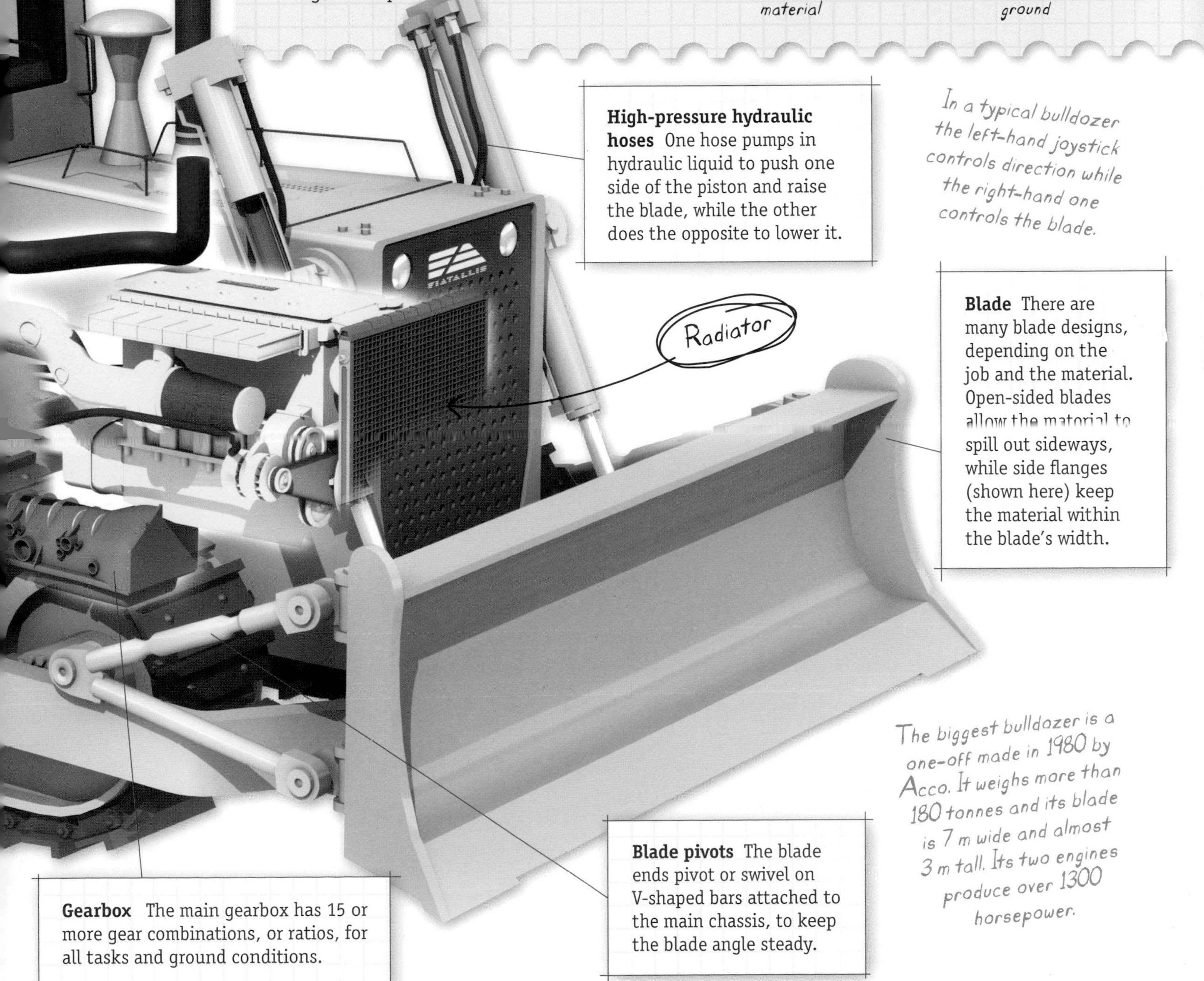

Exhaust

High-pressure hydraulic hoses One hose pumps in hydraulic liquid to push one side of the piston and raise the blade, while the other does the opposite to lower it.

In a typical bulldozer the left-hand joystick controls direction while the right-hand one controls the blade.

Radiator

Blade There are many blade designs, depending on the job and the material. Open-sided blades allow the material to spill out sideways, while side flanges (shown here) keep the material within the blade's width.

The biggest bulldozer is a one-off made in 1980 by Acco. It weighs more than 180 tonnes and its blade is 7 m wide and almost 3 m tall. Its two engines produce over 1300 horsepower.

Blade pivots The blade ends pivot or swivel on V-shaped bars attached to the main chassis, to keep the blade angle steady.

Gearbox The main gearbox has 15 or more gear combinations, or ratios, for all tasks and ground conditions.

BUCKET LOADER

Loading power is vital in mining, construction and other heavy industries – and the front-end loader provides this. Its bucket can lift many tonnes of loose material in one go and tip it where needed – into a trench or dump truck (see page 18), or onto a conveyor belt. Loader buckets are also useful for carrying items such as stacks of building bricks or bundles of timber and lifting them, for example, up onto scaffolding walkways.

Eureka!

Like dumpers and bulldozers, front-end bucket loaders were developed in the 1920s in the USA. The first types were based on farm tractors with a system of cables and winches to raise and tilt the bucket. The first purpose-built version was the Hough HS in 1939.

Whatever next?

Like many giant machines, loaders get bigger and stronger almost every year. There are plans for buckets so big that they could hold more than 300 people.

Giant wheeled loaders (as distinct from caterpillar tracked ones) have tyres more than 4 m tall that weigh 8 tonnes each.

✳ How does ARTICULATED STEERING work?

A long, rigid, one-piece loader chassis is difficult to steer and manoeuvre in restricted places. The articulated loader has a joint between the front bucket and front wheels, and the main body with the engine and rear wheels. This replaces the usual steering system where the wheels themselves turn at an angle. It allows the loader to bend itself into tight corners and line up its bucket neatly with the material it will lift.

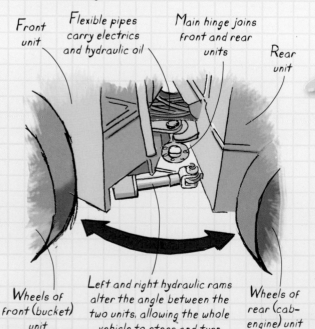

Front unit

Flexible pipes carry electrics and hydraulic oil

Main hinge joins front and rear units

Rear unit

Wheels of front (bucket) unit

Left and right hydraulic rams alter the angle between the two units, allowing the whole vehicle to steer and turn

Wheels of rear (cab-engine) unit

Arm The bucket arm alters the height of the bucket between preset limits, so it cannot go too high and make the loader topple over.

Bucket The volume or capacity of a bucket is usually measured in cubic metres, which is shortened in everyday language to 'metres'.

Bucket ram This hydraulic pusher-puller tilts the bucket, making it face upwards, level or downwards.

Teeth Large teeth along the bucket's lower edge force their way into hard material, such as compacted earth, better than a straight edge.

Watch a video of a bucket loader being put through its paces by visiting www.factsforprojects.com and clicking on the web link.

High-level exhaust Like most big machines with diesel or petrol engines, the exhaust outlet is above the level of the driver, to prevent fumes around the cab.

Le Tourneau's L2350 wheeled loader can lift almost 75 tonnes in one bucket to a height of more than 13 m. with a forward reach of 3.8 m.

Engine housing

FR130

Engine

Floodlights and spotlights Most giant machines have plenty of powerful lights all around, partly for emergency work that has to be done in darkness, as well as to be seen.

The log grab closes its claws on another load of future paper

Fuel tank

Articulated steering This articulated system (see opposite) allows the loader to wriggle in and out of narrow spaces. It is one of more than 12 separate hydraulic systems all over the machine.

* **Lots of LOADING**

A key feature of most loaders is the interchangeable front end. The ordinary bucket can be removed at its standard-sized fitting brackets or lugs, and replaced with any one of a huge variety of sand scoops, bale spikes, log grabs, hooks, pallet forks and similar 'handling' devices. The hydraulic power that controls the tipping bucket is then linked in to work the device, such as opening and closing the arms or claws of the log grab.

Arm ram This hydraulic unit lifts or lowers the arm on which the bucket is mounted. A system of pivoted links between the arm and bucket means that the bucket stays at a constant angle as the arm goes up or comes down.

The 16-cylinder, 65-litre diesel engine in the biggest loaders produces 2300 horsepower.

EARTH SCRAPER

Bulldozers can do some of the work to level an area. But they are slow and their strength may be needed elsewhere on site. So along comes the earth scraper, also called the land plane. It doesn't have the huge pushing power of the bulldozer, so it cannot cope with too many big lumps and bumps. But it is more efficient at earth-moving. One common task is cut-and-fill, which is scraping earth from a high area, leaving it flat, and taking the load to a lower area that needs building up.

Eureka!

Earth scrapers were the brainchild of US engineer-inventor Robert Gilmore LeTourneau, in the 1930s. He was responsible for more than half of the machines and gadgets still in use today in the earth-moving industry.

Whatever next?

As robot drivers, laser systems and satnav (GPS) improve, earth scrapers may become almost entirely automatic. However a human might always be needed in case the robot goes wrong.

The biggest self-powered scrapers have an extra second engine to drive the rear wheels.

Tractor unit The front section pulls along the scraper or hopper. The weight of the engine and cab in front of the wheels balances the load of the hopper to the rear.

Air conditioning The cab's air con unit is on the roof, where the air is least dusty.

Air filter

Laser emits a horizontal laser beam through a rotating aperture (gap)

Hollows or low areas of ground are built up or filled to the level of the laser beam

Bumps or high areas of ground are cut down down by several passes of the earth scraper

✳ How does LASER LEVELLING work?

Lasers are high-energy, powerful beams of light that shine perfectly straight and do not spread out. They are used more and more in heavy engineering and earth-moving, for measuring and checking surfaces. On a large site the laser source is set to exactly the right height and then sends out light pulses that are horizontal and rotate like a lighthouse. Laser sensors on earth scrapers, bulldozers and other earth-movers tell the driver whether each small patch of ground needs to be lower or higher.

Engine A big diesel engine drives the front wheels with a large selection of very slow gears for different terrains.

Off-set cab The driver's cab is next to the engine, with a clear view all along one side of the vehicle for precise steering.

See different models of earth scrapers at work by watching a video. Visit www.factsforprojects.com and click on the web link.

Arm

Hopper Huge amounts of earth can scrape into the hopper, and the blade can be adjusted up or down.

The original invention on which most earth scrapers are based is the Fresno scraper of 1883 from California. It was developed by James Porteous to help dig drainage canals and ditches in the local vineyards.

Blade

Rear wheels The massive rear wheels take the weight of the full hopper. Tyre pressure must be checked because it affects the height of the blade above the ground.

Robert Gilmore LeTourneau's first job was levelling and grading a 16-acre field with a tractor and towed scraper belonging to the local agricultural engineer boss. He opened his first tractor workshop in 1921.

Apron Earth or other material slides into the hopper through the forward-facing gate or apron opening. To unload, a rear hydraulic pusher bar forces it back out again through the gate to the required depth.

Hydraulic steering The hopper is joined to the tractor unit by an articulated steering link (see page 22).

A typical large scraper is 12–15 m long and weighs 40–60 tonnes when fully loaded.

An earth scraper runs to and fro on its cut-and-fill route

✳SMOOTHLY does it

Scrapers and planers are sometimes known as 'graders'. This means they prepare the surface to a certain quality or grade of flatness and slope. Bulldozers and scrapers tend to the rougher or coarser end of grading, although scrapers in particular can cover enormous areas rapidly. For fine grading, with the smoothest finish, the ideal machine is well named – the grader. It is a tractor with a slim, wide blade set low down between the front and rear wheels. This gives the final 'polish' to areas such as sports pitches.

MOBILE CRANE

Cranes are the big lifters among giant machines. Tower cranes stay in one spot, floating cranes are used at sea, while on land, mobile cranes can be transported to where they're needed. Most cranes are carried on huge trucks and weigh more than 100 tonnes. When they hoist a load, the combined weight can be over 500 tonnes. Crane drivers make sure the vehicle is steady and secure before attempting a big lift – and that includes checking the ground underneath.

Eureka!

Simple cranes date back more than 2500 years to ancient Greece. By the time of the Roman Empire they were lifting stone blocks of more than 100 tonnes. Mobile cranes had to wait for the invention of steam engines from the 1800s, and then diesel engines.

The longest crane booms extend more than 100 m, but their loads and also the hoisting speed are strictly limited.

Whatever next?

The world's tallest buildings approach 1000 metres in height, but no tower crane can reach that high. The newest methods allow smaller side cranes to 'piggyback' off the main building.

Boom base The main 'arm' of the crane is called the boom or jib, depending on the design. If it can move up and down, as here, it's called a luffing boom.

The farther a crane boom reaches outwards, the less load it is allowed to lift. A 60-tonne load at 12 m would reduce to 40 tonnes at 15 m.

Swivel joint To traverse, or move the boom to the side, the whole base section of the crane swivels on a rotating platform or turntable.

Crane engine

Drive engines

✳ How do STABILIZERS work?

Most mobile cranes travel on normal highways and so the carrying truck has a limited size. Before the crane starts work, it extends outriggers or stabilizers with legs and feet, to make itself wider at the base. This means the crane cannot topple to the side, especially when it lifts or swings loads in that direction. The truck itself is usually long and heavy enough to prevent toppling in the front-back direction. Gravity and movement sensors warn if the crane starts to lean too much in any direction.

Stabilizers emerge under hydraulic or electric motor power

Crane

Legs lower onto base plate feet to compress the ground

Squashy tyres are lifted off the ground to prevent swaying

Hydraulics Several separate hydraulic systems are used to swivel and luff the crane. If one fails, the machinery locks in a failsafe position to prevent a terrible accident.

Stabilizer legs (retracted)

Multi-wheels Many axles spread the crane's load, which helps to even out the different soft and hard spots in the ground.

View pictures of giant mobile cranes in action by visiting www.factsforprojects.com and clicking on the web link.

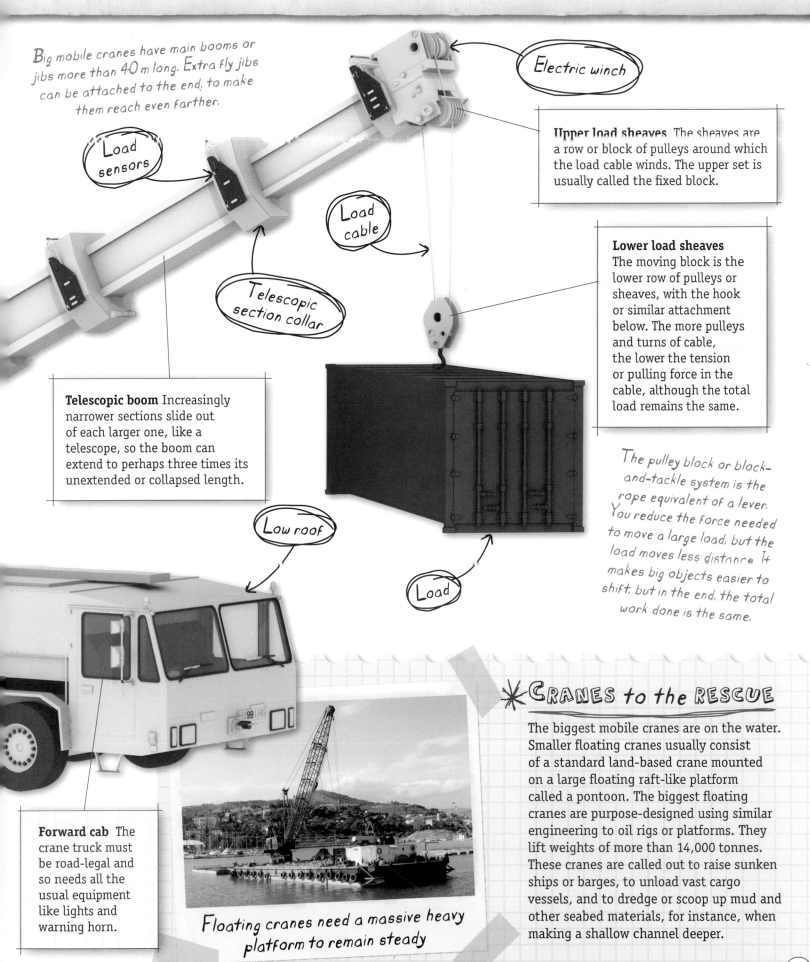

Big mobile cranes have main booms or jibs more than 40 m long. Extra fly jibs can be attached to the end, to make them reach even farther.

Load sensors

Electric winch

Upper load sheaves The sheaves are a row or block of pulleys around which the load cable winds. The upper set is usually called the fixed block.

Load cable

Telescopic section collar

Lower load sheaves The moving block is the lower row of pulleys or sheaves, with the hook or similar attachment below. The more pulleys and turns of cable, the lower the tension or pulling force in the cable, although the total load remains the same.

Telescopic boom Increasingly narrower sections slide out of each larger one, like a telescope, so the boom can extend to perhaps three times its unextended or collapsed length.

The pulley block or block-and-tackle system is the rope equivalent of a lever. You reduce the force needed to move a large load, but the load moves less distance. It makes big objects easier to shift, but in the end, the total work done is the same.

Low roof

Load

Forward cab The crane truck must be road-legal and so needs all the usual equipment like lights and warning horn.

Floating cranes need a massive heavy platform to remain steady

✳ CRANES to the RESCUE

The biggest mobile cranes are on the water. Smaller floating cranes usually consist of a standard land-based crane mounted on a large floating raft-like platform called a pontoon. The biggest floating cranes are purpose-designed using similar engineering to oil rigs or platforms. They lift weights of more than 14,000 tonnes. These cranes are called out to raise sunken ships or barges, to unload vast cargo vessels, and to dredge or scoop up mud and other seabed materials, for instance, when making a shallow channel deeper.

CAR TRANSPORTER

Delivering 10 or 12 cars to the showroom or dealership would be costly if every car had a driver and its own fuel. The transporter packs as many vehicles as possible into its every available corner, with just one driver, and one diesel engine using fuel. The cars arrive fairly clean and with their odometers – the dials or readouts that record mileage travelled – still close to zero.

Eureka!

Multi-vehicle transporters for long-distance travel arrived when mass production by Ford and other car companies took off in the USA in the 1910s. However the most expensive, exclusive car makers still deliver their new products one at a time on a small transporter.

Whatever next?

People who can afford to can now have their new car delievered direct no matter where they are, even on a mountain top. They call a drop-in helicopter service that lowers the vehicle on a cable.

Upper deck After the upper deck is loaded, its rear is raised by the hydraulic struts, and then cars can be driven onto the lower deck.

New vehicles

Hydraulic strut This lowers the rear of the upper deck onto the rear of the lower deck, for loading the upper cars first.

✳ How does the CV JOINT work?

In most vehicles, turning power must be transmitted from the engine in the main body, to the axles and wheels, which move up and down with the suspension. The CV or constant-velocity joint allows this to happen. The drive shaft spun by the engine is connected through the flexible joint to the driven shaft to the wheel. It carries the turning action at the same constant speed (velocity).

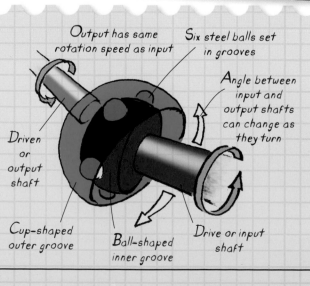

Output has same rotation speed as input

Six steel balls set in grooves

Angle between input and output shafts can change as they turn

Driven or output shaft

Cup-shaped outer groove

Ball-shaped inner groove

Drive or input shaft

Each load of vehicles presents different problems. Vans are tall and need plenty of headroom, while sports cars are low so an extra deck may be fitted.

Read facts and see pictures of how cars are transported by road, rail and sea by visiting www.factsforprojects.com and clicking on the web link.

Apart from delivering new vehicles, transporters also collect them for service or repairs, such as a steering fault recall, that can only be done at a properly equipped factory workshop.

✳ All FULL up

The latest transporters are very adaptable, with decks and ramps that alter length, height and angle. For each delivery, all the vehicle makes and models are fed into a computer program, which calculates their sizes and works out the deck and ramp set-up and loading order. The system also plots the most effective route between several drop-off sites, to save time and fuel.

Every inch of space is used when loading a big transporter

Chocks Small wedges called chocks stop the cars rolling, and they are also tied down using ratchet straps.

Mirrors

Car hire companies use transporters to take cars from a common drop-off point, such as an airport, back to the various pick-up locations.

Tractor unit Various types of tractor unit – cab plus engine – can pull the trailer, provided they have the correct electrical and hydraulic connections.

Fifth wheel The articulated link between the tractor unit and the transporter trailer is known as the 'fifth wheel'. It allows the trailer to manoeuvre easily from side to side.

Sump The oil that lubricates the inside of the engine drains to the sump or oil pan at the base, and is then pumped back around by the oil pump.

Alternator The alternator is driven by the diesel engine and generates electricity for the lights, displays, power steering, servo brakes, hydraulics and other systems.

A transporter's height and width are fed into a route planner that advises the best way to the destination, avoiding low bridges and narrow lanes due to roadworks.

TUNNEL BORING MACHINE

The tunnel boring machine (TBM) is like a giant mechanical worm that drills and scrapes its way through solid rock. It not only cuts into the rock but also sends away the resulting bits and pieces, called spoil, on a conveyor belt or rail wagons. TBMs are controlled by laser guides and other hi-tech systems. This is to ensure that they come out at the other end at exactly the right place.

Eureka!

TBMs were first used in the mid 1800s to cut under the Alps in Europe and make railway tunnels in eastern North America. They were based on lots of small drills, spikes or hammers and were not reliable. The first TBM with a rotary cutting head saw successful action in the 1950s.

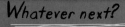

Whatever next?

Adding micro-explosive capsules or pellets to the rotary cutting head can help to soften and shake apart the hardest rock by thousands of tiny blasts every second – provided the cutting head itself can cope.

Japan's Seikan Tunnel, 54 km long and completed in 1988, is the world's longest railway tunnel.

The Channel Tunnel between England and France is 50.5 km in length and drops to a maximum depth of 75 m beneath the Channel.

Conveyer belts Conveyors take the spoil away to the tunnel opening, or to secondary shafts that are dug down from the surface.

Rock

Each of the Channel Tunnel's two main bores is 7.6 m wide.

A massive TBM breaks through to finish off a new tunnel.

Services Electricity cables, hydraulic and pneumatic pipes, ventilation pipes and other supplies trail along behind the TBM.

Linings Prefabricated (already made) sections of collar-like rings are installed as soon as it is practically possible, to stop the tunnel walls breaking.

✳ WORM or MOLE?

A TBM has features in common with a burrowing earthworm and a digging mole. It extends itself using propulsion jacks to force its way along a small distance, then shortens and moves bodily forwards, like a worm. The cutting head has ultra-hard teeth that scratch and scrape like a mole's front claws. Behind the TBM, more machines add ready-made curved lining sections onto the tunnel walls, or spray concrete-like mixtures that soon harden, to prevent collapse and cave-ins.

The Channel Tunnel's TBMs were drilled into a side tunnel and left behind when the tunnel was complete.

Go to www.factsforprojects.com and click on the web link to discover facts, videos and pictures about the Niagara Tunnel Project.

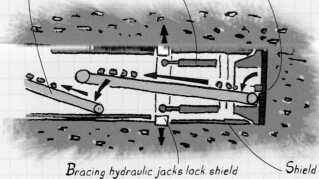

Conveyors carry away spoil

Propulsion hydraulic jacks push cutting head forwards

Cutting head rotates

Bracing hydraulic jacks lock shield against walls while tunnelling

Shield

✳ How do TBMs and CUTTING HEADS work?

The TMB's shield is a metal cylinder with the cutting head at the front. The head's one or more toothed wheels turn or rotate slowly with enormous power to grind the rock. Loosened spoil falls onto a collecting conveyor for removal. The shield is held against the walls by bracing hydraulic jacks so that propulsion jacks can push the cutting head into the rock. After a time, the bracing jacks loosen, the propulsion jacks shorten, the whole TBM moves forwards and the process starts again.

Bracing jacks These push sideways against the tunnel wall, so that as the propulsion jacks press the cutting head forwards, the shield does not slide backwards.

Shield The main boring machinery is housed in this large casing, which helps to keep most particles of rock away from the moving parts.

Cutting head The head or wheel turns at a slow and steady rate, perhaps once every few seconds. Its size determines the diameter or width of the tunnel.

Propulsion jacks These are hydraulic rams that force the cutting head forwards against the rock. They respond and adjust their pressure to the rock's varying hardness.

Rock Different types of rock have very different hardness and consistency. Narrow test drills in front of the main bore help to warn engineers about conditions ahead.

NASA CRAWLER TRANSPORTER

The world's largest self-powered tracked vehicles are two crawler-transporters at the USA's Kennedy Space Centre, Florida. They carry mobile launch platforms with rockets or space shuttles on top, from the vast assembly building where they are put together and prepared, out to the launch area. The crawler moves away before the rocket or shuttle blasts from the platform on its immense journey.

Eureka!

Early in its space programme the US decided to assemble its rockets in an upright position and move them like this to the launch area. This got around the problem of putting together a huge rocket lying down and then having to tip it upright.

Whatever next?

The crawlers have been on duty since the 1960s. They have many more missions to come as the US readies its replacements for the shuttles, known as Ares rockets.

The crawlers come back from the launch area with their empty platforms at just over 3 km/hour, which is twice as fast as they travel on the outward trip.

✳ SNAIL'S pace

The crawler-transporter must travel very slowly with its tall, weighty and possibly wobby load. The whole shuttle set-up with the white orbiter spaceplane, the huge bullet-shaped brown fuel tank (empty) and two white rocket boosters weighs more than 1200 tonnes, and the mobile launch platform it sits on is 3700 tonnes! The crawler's top speed loaded is just 1.5 kilometres per hour. So the average trip from the assembly building to the launch area takes more than five hours.

Generators The two Alco propulsion diesel engines turn four generators, each producing 1000 kilowatts, for the total of 16 electrical traction engines.

Laser-controlled hydraulic jacks alter the angle of the launch platform.

Gantry

Traction motor

The massive crawler slowly makes its way to the launch site

The whole crawler vehicle is 40 m wide and 35 m long and weighs 2400 tonnes.

Shoes Each shoe weighs almost one tonne and there are 57 in each crawler track.

For lots of close-up pictures of the crawler transporter go to www.factsforprojects.com and click on the web link.

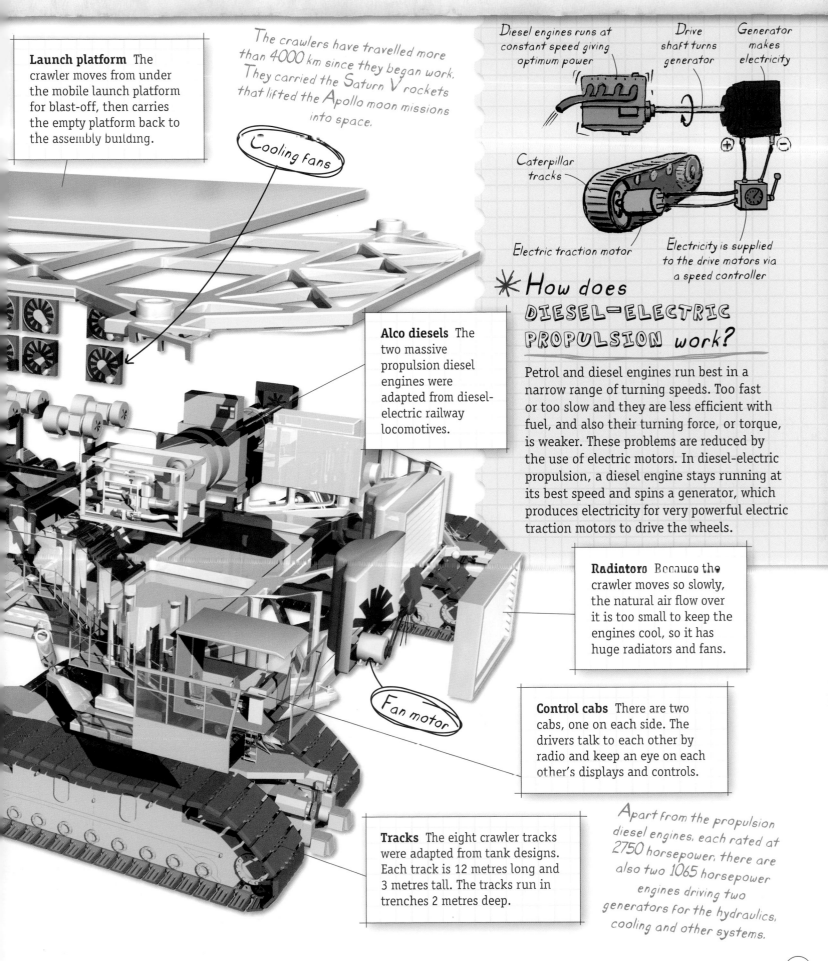

Launch platform The crawler moves from under the mobile launch platform for blast-off, then carries the empty platform back to the assembly building.

The crawlers have travelled more than 4000 km since they began work. They carried the Saturn V rockets that lifted the Apollo moon missions into space.

Cooling fans

Diesel engines runs at constant speed giving optimum power

Drive shaft turns generator

Generator makes electricity

Caterpillar tracks

Electric traction motor

Electricity is supplied to the drive motors via a speed controller

Alco diesels The two massive propulsion diesel engines were adapted from diesel-electric railway locomotives.

✳ How does **DIESEL-ELECTRIC PROPULSION** work?

Petrol and diesel engines run best in a narrow range of turning speeds. Too fast or too slow and they are less efficient with fuel, and also their turning force, or torque, is weaker. These problems are reduced by the use of electric motors. In diesel-electric propulsion, a diesel engine stays running at its best speed and spins a generator, which produces electricity for very powerful electric traction motors to drive the wheels.

Radiators Because the crawler moves so slowly, the natural air flow over it is too small to keep the engines cool, so it has huge radiators and fans.

Fan motor

Control cabs There are two cabs, one on each side. The drivers talk to each other by radio and keep an eye on each other's displays and controls.

Tracks The eight crawler tracks were adapted from tank designs. Each track is 12 metres long and 3 metres tall. The tracks run in trenches 2 metres deep.

Apart from the propulsion diesel engines, each rated at 2750 horsepower, there are also two 1065 horsepower engines driving two generators for the hydraulics, cooling and other systems.

BUCKET WHEEL EXCAVATOR

Our modern world is hungry for energy and materials such as metals and chemicals. Most of these come from the Earth itself. Coal and valuable metal- and mineral-bearing rocks are mined, quarried, drilled, dug and excavated from the surface by massive machines. The bucket-wheel excavator is the most gigantic of all. It crawls along and 'eats' into the soil and rocks, moving hundreds of tonnes with just one turn of its big wheel.

Eureka!

Mining went mechanical hundreds of years ago, with stone or iron hammers on wooden levers smashing into the area being mined. As the Industrial Revolution got under way in the 1700s it brought steam-powered excavators fuelled by the coal they were digging out.

Whatever next?

Already the biggest vehicles ever made, bucket-wheel excavators may grow even larger to cope with demands from today's industry. But they will probably be built and moved to the site as separate parts, then fitted together.

Really big excavators take four years to build and need a crew of five or six operators. They can dig out more than 200,000 tonnes of coal or ore every day.

Frame The main frame is made of massive steel beams and girders welded together. The design basics are a combination of oil rigs and huge cranes.

Counterweight The long arm with the bucket wheel at its end puts enormous strain on the main vehicle. It is balanced or countered by a large container or hopper filled with spoil.

Cooling fans

Secondary unit The secondary crawler at the end of the second conveyor can be positioned to tip its material into waiting dump trucks, train wagons, another conveyor or onto a storage pile.

Bucket wheel rotates

Material falls onto conveyor

Work face

Buckets gouge out huge amounts

More conveyors carry the material away

✳ How do BUCKET WHEELS work?

The excavator's wheel rotates slowly as it moves into the rock, carried on the vast arm which swivels on the main vehicle. The sharp-edged buckets gnaw and nibble into the work face (see above), loosening and collecting pieces. As the buckets turn up and over, the material falls onto the conveyor. After one arm swivel, the whole machine moves along on its crawler tracks and repeats the action.

Watch a video of a bucket wheel excavator at work by visiting www.factsforprojects.com and clicking on the website.

✳ Enormous APPETITES

Huge excavators work tirelessly day and night, scraping away ever-deeper layers as they creep across the landscape. They remove entire habitats of plants and animals, leaving behind bare soil or rocks. Modern quarrying and mining methods aim to replace the natural scenery by covering with earth, planting new trees and flowers, and bringing back the original creatures. This may happen after the empty area is filled with unwanted material, or spoil, from mines elswehere.

A giant excavator gulps up huge loads leaving the area bare

Crane

The German Takraf Bagger 293 holds the record as the largest-ever land vehicle. It is 200 m long and 96 m tall, and weighs 14,000 tonnes.

Buckets The bucket teeth and edges are made of ultra-hard metals such as titanium alloys, but even so, they need replacing often.

Conveyor

The largest bucket wheels measure more than 20 m across. Each bucket holds up to 15 cubic m – about the same amount as 100 bathtubs.

Transformers These take supplied electricity and alter it for the motors that turn the bucket wheel, conveyor belts and crawler tracks.

Gantries Walkways and gantries allow people to reach most of the working parts, for regular safety checks and repairs.

Caterpillar tracks The tracks only need to move very slowly, perhaps just 2 or 3 metres per minute, once the excavator is on site. However this means that travelling to new areas might take several weeks.

LONDON EYE

The UK's most popular paying tourist attraction is the London Eye, also known as the Millennium Wheel, on the south bank of the river Thames in central London. Built to mark the Millennium celebrations, and opened to the public in the year 2000, it is Europe's biggest 'entertainment wheel' and third-largest in the world. To emphasize the high up-and-over action of the trips or rides, they are known as 'flights'.

Eureka!

Theme park wheels or 'big wheels' are often known as ferris wheels after bridge designer George Ferris. He built the first working version in Chicago, USA in the 1890s for the World's Columbian Exposition. It was 80 metres tall.

Whatever next?

Since its opening the London Eye has been overtaken by taller wheels, first in Nanchang, China, then Singapore. The soon-to-be opened Beijing Great Wheel, also in China, will be bigger too, and opens in 2010.

Each flight or rotation takes about 30 minutes, with up to 800 passengers if all the capsules are full.

Peak times for London Eye trips are booked many weeks in advance. You can just turn up, but you might have a wait of several hours!

✳ What a FLIGHT!

Apart from St Paul's Cathedral towards the eastern side of central London, the city had no high-level observation areas for the public. This was one of the main ideas behind the London Eye. Passengers can see all the major landmarks including the Houses of Parliament, Buckingham Palace, Tower Bridge, and the skyscrapers of the City of London including the 'Gherkin', and beyond into Docklands. On a clear day the view extends for 40 kilometres, far beyond the city to the North Downs towards the south.

Spoke cables These 64 cables work by tension, or pull, only. They have little pushing strength, like the spokes of a bicycle wheel.

Hub and spindle The spindle is 23 metres long and the hub turns on it using massive bearings. The spindle and hub together weigh 330 tonnes, and the whole London Eye, with capsules, has a total weight of 2100 tonnes.

Around 3.5 million people 'fly the Eye' every year.

Stairs

Drive wheels The wheel is rim-driven by friction, or rubbing. Lorry tyres turned by electric motors press onto the rim and make it move along.

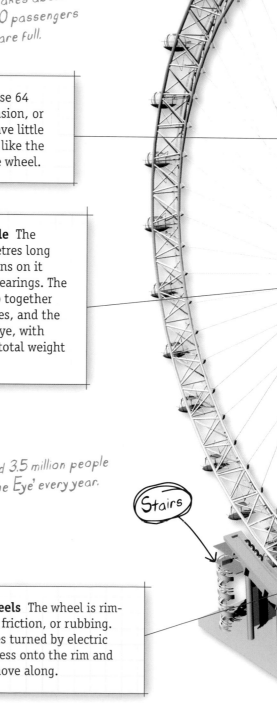

Tourists enjoy a view of the Big Ben clock tower at the top of a flight

Experience 360° views of the London Eye and surrounding area by visiting www.factsforprojects.com and clicking on the website.

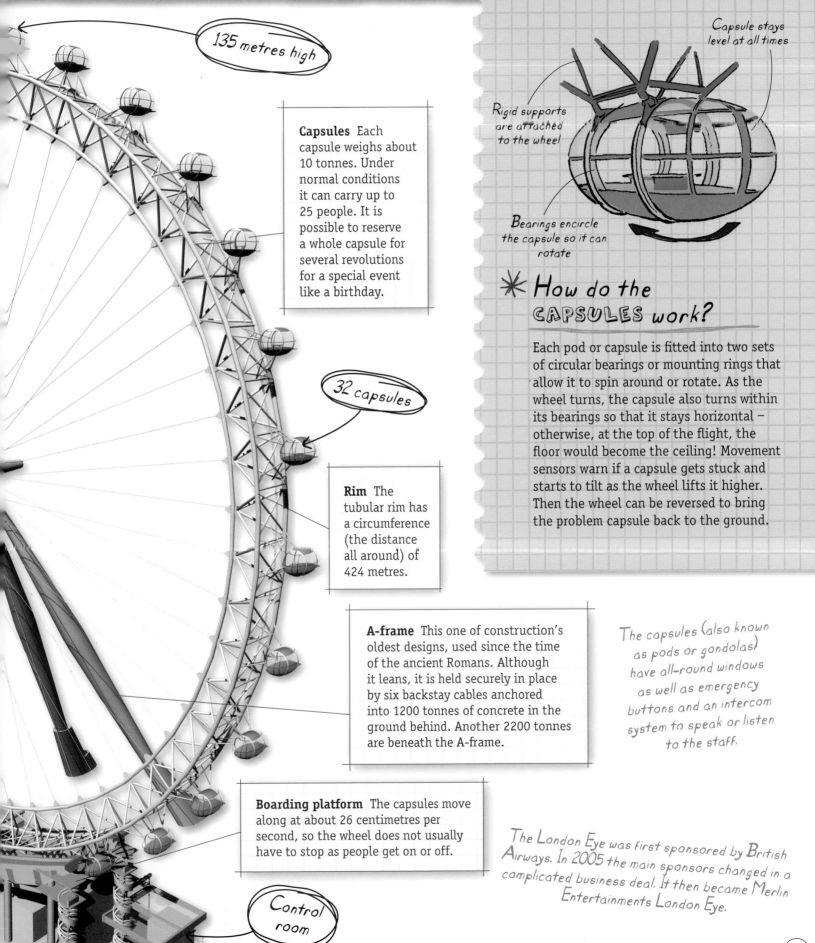

135 metres high

Capsules Each capsule weighs about 10 tonnes. Under normal conditions it can carry up to 25 people. It is possible to reserve a whole capsule for several revolutions for a special event like a birthday.

32 capsules

Rim The tubular rim has a circumference (the distance all around) of 424 metres.

A-frame This one of construction's oldest designs, used since the time of the ancient Romans. Although it leans, it is held securely in place by six backstay cables anchored into 1200 tonnes of concrete in the ground behind. Another 2200 tonnes are beneath the A-frame.

Boarding platform The capsules move along at about 26 centimetres per second, so the wheel does not usually have to stop as people get on or off.

Control room

Capsule stays level at all times

Rigid supports are attached to the wheel

Bearings encircle the capsule so it can rotate

✳ How do the CAPSULES work?

Each pod or capsule is fitted into two sets of circular bearings or mounting rings that allow it to spin around or rotate. As the wheel turns, the capsule also turns within its bearings so that it stays horizontal – otherwise, at the top of the flight, the floor would become the ceiling! Movement sensors warn if a capsule gets stuck and starts to tilt as the wheel lifts it higher. Then the wheel can be reversed to bring the problem capsule back to the ground.

The capsules (also known as pods or gondolas) have all-round windows as well as emergency buttons and an intercom system to speak or listen to the staff.

The London Eye was first sponsored by British Airways. In 2005 the main sponsors changed in a complicated business deal. It then became Merlin Entertainments London Eye.

GLOSSARY

Alloy
A combination of metals, or metals and other substances, for special purposes such as great strength, extreme lightness, resistance to high temperatures, or all of these.

Articulated
In vehicles, having a joint or bendy part rather than being stiff and rigid all the way along.

Bearing
A part designed for efficient movement, to reduce friction and wear, for example, between a spinning shaft or axle and its frame.

Boom
A long, slim, arm-like part, sometimes called a jib, of a crane or similar machine that can usually move up and down, from side to side and perhaps in and out.

Chassis
The main structural framework or 'skeleton' of a vehicle, that gives it strength, and to which other parts are fixed, like the engine and seats.

Con-rod
Connecting rod, an engine part that links the piston to the main crankshaft.

Constant-velocity (CV) joint
A mechanical joint or linkage that carries a turning action from one part to the other at the same regular (or constant) speed (velocity).

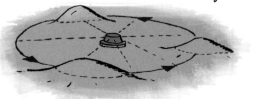
Laser levelling

Power take-off

Crankshaft
The main turning shaft in an engine, which is made to rotate by the up-and-down movements of the pistons.

Cylinder
In an engine or mechanical part, the chamber inside which a well-fitting piston moves.

Damper
A part that reduces or dampens movements, usually sudden jolts or to-and-fro vibrations. On vehicle suspensions it is sometimes called the shock-absorber.

Diesel engine
An internal combustion engine (one that burns or combusts fuel inside a chamber, the cylinder), which uses diesel fuel, and causes this to explode by pressure alone rather than by a spark plug.

Differential
A part that makes road wheels turn at different speeds as a vehicle goes round a bend. The wheel on the outside of the curve must spin slightly faster because it has farther to go than the inner wheel and would otherwise judder or skid.

Drive shaft
A spinning shaft from an engine or motor that drives or powers another part, such as the propeller of a water vessel or the caterpillar tracks of a bulldozer.

Friction
When two objects rub or scrape together, causing wear and losing movement energy by turning it into sound and heat.

Fuel
A substance with lots of energy in the form of its matter or substance, as chemical energy. We usually release this energy for use by burning. In some cases fuels are used in other ways – in a fuel cell, hydrogen fuel is converted into electricity.

Gears
Toothed wheels or sprockets that fit or mesh together so that one turns the other. If they are connected by a chain or belt with holes where the teeth fit, they are generally called sprockets. Gears are used to change turning speed and force, for example, between an engine and the road wheels of a vehicle, or to change the direction of rotation.

Tunnel boring machine
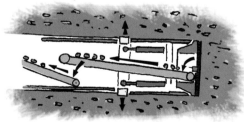

Generator
A machine that changes kinetic or mechanical energy – the energy of movement – into electricity.

GPS
Global Positioning System, a network of more than 20 satellites in space going around the Earth. They send out radio signals about their position and the time, allowing people to find their location using GPS receivers or 'satnavs'.

Gravity

The natural pulling force or attraction that all objects have, no matter what their size. Bigger or more massive objects have more gravity than smaller ones.

Hydraulic

Working by high-pressure liquid such as oil or water.

Jib

The arm or boom of a crane that angles forwards or horizontally.

Laser

A special high-energy form of light which is only one pure colour, where all the waves are exactly the same length, and they are parallel to each other rather than spreading out as in normal light.

Luff

To raise up and lower down in a vertical direction, as with the boom or jib of a crane.

Petrol engine

An internal combustion engine (one that burns or combusts fuel inside a chamber, the cylinder) that uses petrol fuel and causes this to explode using a spark plug.

Piston

A wide, rod-shaped part, similar in shape to a food or drinks can, that moves along or up and down inside a close-fitting chamber, the cylinder.

Bucket wheel excavator

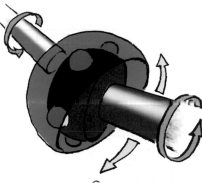

Constant velocity joint

Pneumatic

Working by high-pressure gas such as air or oxygen.

Radiator

In cars and similar vehicles, a part designed to lose heat, for example, from an engine. It has a large surface area, usually lots of fins or vanes. Hot water from the engine circulates through it, to become cooler before flowing back to the engine.

Radio

Signals and messages sent by invisible waves of combined electricity and magnetism, where each wave is quite long, from a few millimetres to many kilometres. (Light waves are similar but much shorter.)

Satellite

Any object that goes around or orbits another. For example, the Moon is a natural satellite of the Earth. The term is used especially for artificial or man-made orbiting objects, particularly those going around the Earth.

Satnav

Satellite navigation, finding your way and location using radio signals from the GPS (Global Positioning System) satellites in space.

Suspension

Parts that allow the road wheels or tracks of a vehicle to move up and down separately from the driver and passengers, to smooth out bumps and dips in the road. Also any similar system that gives a softer, more comfortable ride.

Telescopic

When one part or section of a structure slides inside another, as in a telescope, an extending ladder or certain kinds of cranes.

Articulated steering

Turbo

Using a turbine, which is a set of angled fan-like blades on a spinning shaft, found in many areas of engineering, from pumps and cars to jet engines.

Winch

A winding mechanism that turns or reels in a rope or cable, slowly but with great force.

London Eye

INDEX